TIME ZONES

WORKBOOK | THIRD EDITION

CARMELLA LIESKE

NATIONAL GEOGRAPHIC
LEARNING

Australia · Brazil · Mexico · Singapore · United Kingdom · United States

NATIONAL GEOGRAPHIC LEARNING

National Geographic Learning,
a Cengage Company

Time Zones Workbook 1 Third Edition

Carmella Lieske

Publisher: Andrew Robinson

Managing Editor: Derek Mackrell

Additional Editorial Support: Melissa Pang,
   Sarah Jane Lewis

Director of Global Marketing: Ian Martin

Senior Product Marketing Manager: Anders Bylund

Heads of Regional Marketing:
   Charlotte Ellis (Europe, Middle East and Africa)
   Kiel Hamm (Asia)
   Irina Pereyra (Latin America)

Senior Production Controller: Tan Jin Hock

Associate Media Researcher: Jeffrey Millies

Senior Designer: Lisa Trager

Operations Support: Rebecca G. Barbush,
   Hayley Chwazik-Gee

Manufacturing Planner: Mary Beth Hennebury

Composition: Symmetry Creative Production, Inc.

For permission to use material from this text or product, submit all requests online at **cengage.com/permissions** Further permissions questions can be emailed to **permissionrequest@cengage.com**

ISBN-13: 978-0-357-42637-1

National Geographic Learning
200 Pier 4 Boulevard
Boston, MA 02210
USA

Locate your local office at **international.cengage.com/region**

Visit National Geographic Learning online at **ELTNGL.com**
Visit our corporate website at **www.cengage.com**

CONTENTS

UNIT 1
What's Your Favorite Video Game? 4

UNIT 2
This Place Is Amazing! 10

UNIT 3
Where's the Lion? 16

UNIT 4
This Is My Family 22

UNIT 5
I Like Fruit! 28

UNIT 6
What Time Does Class Start? 34

UNIT 7
Can Elephants Swim? 40

UNIT 8
How Much Is That T-Shirt? 46

UNIT 9
What Are You Doing? 52

UNIT 10
What's the Weather Like? 58

UNIT 11
I Went to Australia! 64

UNIT 12
What Did You Do For New Year's? 70

Language Notes 76

Photo and Art Credits 80

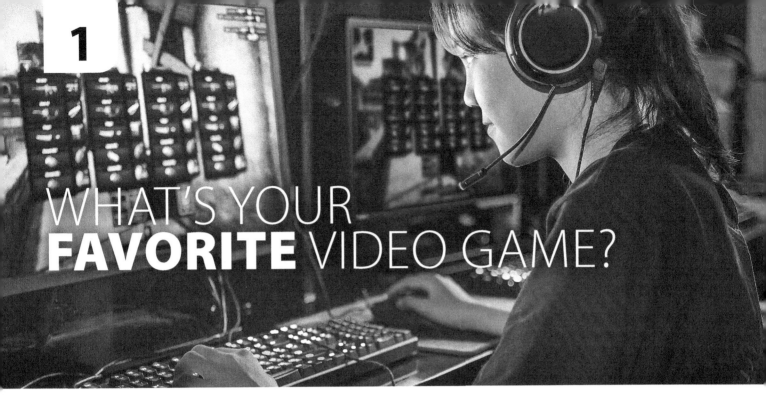

1 WHAT'S YOUR FAVORITE VIDEO GAME?

PREVIEW

A Label the pictures. Use the words in the box.

> video game   movie   app   singer   TV show   ~~writer~~

1 w r i t e r

2 _ _ _ _ _

3 _ _ _ _ _ _ _ _ _ _

4 _ _ _ _ _ _

5 _ _ _

6 _ _ _ _ _ _

B Write. Put the words from **A** in alphabetical order (**a**, **b**, **c** …).

1 _app_

2 _____

3 _____

4 _____

5 _____

6 _____

C Complete the chart. Use the words from **A**.

Person	Thing
writer	app

LANGUAGE FOCUS

A **Complete the conversations.** Circle the correct answers.

1 **Claire:** What's **her / your** favorite video game?

   Sam: My favorite video game is *League of Legends*.

2 **Isabella:** What's his favorite music app?

   Jack: **His / Their** favorite music app is Spotify.

3 **Diego:** **Who's / What's** her favorite singer?

   Jenny: Lady Gaga.

4 **Maria:** What's your favorite season?

   Peng: **My / Their** favorite season is spring.

5 **Tammy:** What's **his / her** favorite movie?

   Ying: *Incredibles 2*. She loves it!

6 **Luka:** **Who's / What's** their favorite color?

   Ben: Their favorite color is red.

B **Look at the chart.** Answer the questions.

	Jennifer	Matt
Favorite color	green	white
Favorite video game	*Tomb Raider*	*World of Warcraft*
Favorite movie	*Aladdin*	*Star Wars*
Favorite singer	Bruno Mars	Ed Sheeran

1 What's Jennifer's favorite color? _Her favorite color is green._

2 What's her favorite movie? _____

3 Who's her favorite singer? _____

4 What's Matt's favorite video game? _____

5 What's his favorite color? _____

6 What's his favorite movie? _____

C **Match.** Join the two parts of the conversation.

1 What's his favorite season?   ○   ○ **a** Their favorite movie is *Toy Story 4*.

2 What's your favorite book?   ○   ○ **b** Spotify.

3 What's their favorite movie?   ○   ○ **c** Spring.

4 What's her favorite music app?   ○   ○ **d** My favorite book is *On the Come Up*.

THE WORLD'S FAVORITE SPORTS

A **Label the pictures.** Use the words in the box.

> basketball   table tennis   soccer   baseball

1 _____

2 _____

3 _____

4 _____

B **Complete the chart.** Use the countries in the box.

> the United States   Brazil   Japan   China

Asia	North America	South America

C **Read the sentences.** Circle **T** for true or **F** for False.

1 Baseball is the favorite sport in China.   **T**   **F**

2 Basketball is a popular sport in the United States.   **T**   **F**

3 Many people in Brazil like soccer.   **T**   **F**

READING

A **Skim the article.** Who is it about? _____

MY FAVORITE ...

Hi! My name is Francisco. I'm 14. I'm from São Paulo in Brazil. My favorite sport is soccer. My favorite team is Real Madrid from Spain. My favorite sports
5 star is Eden Hazard. He's from Belgium. He's a soccer player.

My favorite movie star is Chris Evans. He's from the United States. My favorite movie is *Captain America*. My favorite
10 video game is *Marvel's Avengers*. My favorite singer is Lady Gaga.

B **Answer the questions about *My Favorite ...***

1 MAIN IDEA What's the article about?

   a hobbies   **b** favorites   **c** free time

2 DETAIL How old is Francisco?

   a 14 years old   **b** 15 years old   **c** 16 years old

3 DETAIL Where is Eden Hazard from?

   a Belgium   **b** the United States   **c** Brazil

4 REFERENCE The word *He's* in line 8 refers to _____.

   a Francisco   **b** Eden Hazard   **c** Chris Evans

5 DETAIL *Marvel's Avengers* is Francisco's favorite _____.

   a movie   **b** video game   **c** app

C **EXAM PRACTICE** **Answer the questions.** Choose no more than two words from the article for each answer.

1 Francisco is from _____.

2 _____ is Francisco's favorite soccer team.

3 Lady Gaga is Francisco's _____.

VOCABULARY

A **Complete the sentences.** Circle the correct answers.

1 That's my favorite TV show. I **love / interesting** it.

2 I want to **watch / travel** to Brazil.

3 I **watch / difficult** movies on Saturday.

4 I'm not good at table tennis. It's **easy / difficult** for me.

5 I really like math. It's **love / easy**.

6 English is a(n) **travel / interesting** class for me.

B **Read the sentences below.** Write the underlined words in the chart.

1 This is <u>exciting</u>! I love baseball.

2 I want to <u>travel</u> to Africa.

3 Some people think science is <u>difficult</u>.

4 What's a popular music <u>app</u>?

5 Many people play <u>table tennis</u>.

6 The Marvel movies are <u>interesting</u>.

7 My favorite color <u>is</u> black.

8 <u>China</u> is in Asia.

9 His books <u>are</u> amazing.

Nouns	Verbs	Adjectives

WRITING

Sentences and questions always start with a capital letter (**W**, **M**, etc.).

A Read the information.

Questions end with a question mark (**?**).

What's your favorite movie**?**

capital letter   **question mark**

Most sentences end with a period (**.**).

My favorite movie is *Avengers: Endgame***.**

capital letter   **period**

Sentences with exciting or surprising things end with an exclamation point (**!**).

The Avengers is my favorite movie, too**!**

capital letter   **exclamation point**

B Complete the chart. What are your favorite things?

Favorite Color	Favorite Day of the Week	Favorite Video Game
Favorite Singer	**Favorite Movie**	**Favorite Sports Player**

C Write sentences about your favorite things. Use your notes from B.

_____

_____

_____

_____

_____

2

THIS PLACE IS AMAZING!

PREVIEW

A Unscramble the words.

1 e s a   _ _e_ _

2 a h e c b   _ _ _ _ _h_

3 n i i d u b g l _b_ _i_ _ _ _ _ _ _

4 e t e t r s   _t_ _ _ _ _ _ _

5 t e r s o   _ _ _o_ _ _

6 c y t i   _ _ _ _y_

B Label the pictures. Use the words from **A**.

1 _ _sea_ _   2 _ _ _ _ _   3 _ _ _ _ _   4 _ _ _ _ _   5 _ _ _ _ _   6 _ _ _ _ _

C Write. Answer the questions.

1 What places from **A** are there in your city? _____

2 What's your favorite city? _____

LANGUAGE FOCUS

A **Complete the sentences.** Circle the correct answers.

1 Xi'an **is** / **are** very old.

2 The museums **are** / **aren't** small. They're big.

3 The buildings in Copenhagen **are** / **is** colorful.

4 **Their** / **They're** amazing!

5 The **street** / **streets** are beautiful.

6 They **'re not** / **'s not** famous.

B **Correct the mistake in each conversation.**

1 **Sam:** Is your house new?

Ying: ~~Yes~~ No, it's not.

2 **Claire:** Is Polihale Beach in Hawaii amazing?

Luka: Yes, they is.

3 **Jack:** Are your city clean?

Maria: Yes, it is.

4 **Tammy:** Is the store famous?

Diego: No, it aren't.

5 **Peng:** Are these streets popular?

Jenny: No, they are. Tourists love them!

6 **Isabella:** Is the design of the Louvre Museum interesting?

Ben: Yes, it are.

C **Rewrite the sentences.** Use the words in the box.

> isn't   aren't   isn't   they're   ~~it's~~

1 It is not very clean. _It's not very clean_____.

2 The style is not popular. _____.

3 The designs are not new. _____.

4 It is not very famous. _____.

5 They are very colorful. _____.

WONDERS OF THE WORLD

Let's look at three more places we call Wonders of the World.

1 This is the Colosseum. It's in Rome, Italy. It's 50 meters tall. It's almost 2,000 years old.

2 This is El Castillo in Chichén Itzá, in Mexico. It's 24 meters tall. It's at least 1,000 years old.

3 This is Christ the Redeemer in Brazil. It's on a mountain. It's 30 meters tall. It's about 100 years old.

A Match. Join each place to the continent it is in.

1 Colosseum ○   ○ **a** North America

2 El Castillo ○   ○ **b** South America

3 Christ the Redeemer ○   ○ **c** Europe

B Write. Put the three places from the article in the correct order.

1 tall → taller → tallest

	Christ the Redeemer	

2 old → → new

READING

A **Skim the article.** What is it about?

  a hotels   **b** towns   **c** countries

UNUSUAL PLACES

Buesingen on the High Rhine is a small town. It's a German town, but it's in Switzerland! Germany is not far away—only 0.8 kilometers. Many tourists go to the town.
5 Some enjoy the river and the waterfalls. They get the best of Germany and the best of Switzerland!

Matmata is a small town in Tunisia. Some people live underground. The buildings in
10 Matmata are famous in movies. The Hotel Sidi Driss is Luke Skywalker's house in the *Star Wars* movies. Because the buildings are underground, the houses aren't cold in the winter.

Buesingen

B **EXAM PRACTICE** **Complete the summary.** Use the words in the box.

> tourists   Switzerland   amazing
> hotel   German

Buesingen on the High Rhine is famous. It is

1 _____ , but it's in

2 _____ . Matmata is famous,

too. A 3 _____ there is in a

popular movie. 4 _____

like to go to both places. The towns are

5 _____ for different reasons.

Matmata

C **Answer the question.**

Do you want to go to Buesingen or Matmata? _____

VOCABULARY

A Label the pictures. Use the words in the box.

| boat | hotel | island | restaurant | tourists | ~~town~~ |

1 _____ town _____

2 _____

3 _____

4 _____

5 _____

6 _____

B Complete the sentences. Circle the correct answers.

1 There are houses **and** / **but** stores in Buesingen on the High Rhine.

2 The restaurant is famous **and** / **but** popular.

3 I love skateboarding, **and** / **but** it's very difficult!

4 Some tourists enjoy the waterfalls **and** / **but** the river.

5 That hotel isn't great, **and** / **but** the food in the restaurant is good.

WRITING

WRITING TIP **Parts of a sentence**

Sentences usually have three main parts: the subject, the verb, and a description.

A Read the information.

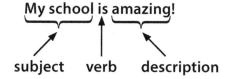

My school is amazing!

subject   verb   description

subject: **My school**

verb: **is**

description (of person or thing): **amazing**

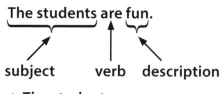

The students are fun.

subject   verb   description

subject: **The students**

verb: **are**

description (of person or thing): **fun**

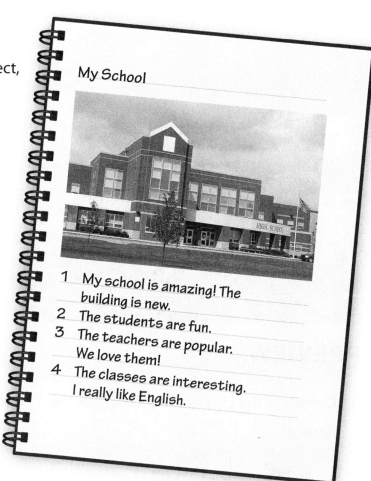

My School

1 My school is amazing! The building is new.
2 The students are fun.
3 The teachers are popular. We love them!
4 The classes are interesting. I really like English.

B What's your favorite place? Complete the chart with your ideas.

Favorite place	
Description of favorite place	
People at that place	
Description of people	
Things in that place	
Description of things	

C Write sentences about your favorite place. Use your notes from **B**.

1 _____

2 _____

3 _____

4 _____

5 _____

6 _____

WHERE'S THE LION?

PREVIEW

A   Complete the crossword puzzle. Use the pictures to help you.

Across

3

4

7

8

10

Down

1

2

5

6

9

B   Complete the chart. Use the words from **A**.

Animals on land	Animals in the water	Animals on land and in the water
giraffe	shark	

LANGUAGE FOCUS

A Look at the picture below. Circle **T** for True or **F** for False.

1 The frogs are on the tree.   T   F

2 The hippo is in the water.   T   F

3 The elephant is under the tree.   T   F

4 There's an elephant in the water.   T   F

5 There are three fish in the water.   T   F

6 There are monkeys next to the rock.   T   F

B Complete the questions. Write one word.

1 _____Where_____ are the monkeys?

2 _____ many frogs are there?

3 Where _____ the elephant?

4 _____ the hippo in the water?

5 _____ the frogs next to the monkeys?

C Write. Look at the picture in **A**. Answer the questions in **B**.

1 They're on the rock. _____

2 _____

3 _____

4 _____

5 _____

LIFE IN ANTARCTICA

A Gentoo penguin stands on the ice at Cuverville Island, Antarctica.

A leopard seal swims near Astrolabe Island, Antarctica.

	Colors	Weight	Size	Favorite food
Leopard seal	black, gray	about 380 kg	about 3.5 m	penguins
Gentoo penguin	white, black	about 5 kg	about 0.7 m	fish

A Look at the chart. Answer the questions.

1 Which animal is big? _____

2 Which animal is long? _____

3 Which animal is white? _____

4 Leopard seals' favorite food is _____.

5 Gentoo penguins like _____.

B Write. What word can you use to describe each animal?

_____

READING

A Look at the photos. What are they?

  a rocks   **b** sea animals   **c** seaweed

WHAT IS IT?

Do you know what this is? It's a cuttlefish. It's like an octopus. The cuttlefish is an amazing animal. It changes color to hide. In the sand, it is the color of sand. In seaweed, it is the color of seaweed.

What do you think this is? It's a mimic octopus. It changes colors to look like different animals. Sometimes it looks like a scary snake and sometimes it looks like a fish.

B Read *What is it?*. Complete the diagram. Use the descriptions (**a–f**) in the box.

  a ~~lives in the sea~~

  b sometimes looks like a different animal

  c sometimes looks like the color of sand

  d changes color

  e sometimes looks like a fish

  f sometimes looks like the color of seaweed

cuttlefish   mimic octopus

a

C   **EXAM PRACTICE**   **Complete the sentences.** Choose no more than three words from the passage in **A** for each answer.

  1 A cuttlefish is like _____.

  2 A _____ looks like the colors it is near.

  3 A _____ looks like different animals.

VOCABULARY

A **Complete the sentences.** Circle the correct answers.

1 The cheetah can **hide** / **change** in the long grass.

2 A mother rabbit keeps her babies warm with her **branches** / **body**.

3 Is my new book **leaves** / **the same as** yours?

4 Do you eat **seaweed** / **hide** in your country?

5 Some birds are sitting on the **branches** / **seaweed** of that tree.

6 Many trees lose their **body** / **leaves** in the winter.

B **Look at the picture below.** Complete the sentences. Use the words in the box.

> on the left   in the middle   on the right

1 The shark is _____ .

2 The fish are _____ .

3 The seaweed is _____ .

WRITING

WRITING TIP Using *a* and *an*

A   Read the information.

Use *an* before words that start with a vowel sound
(*a*, *e*, *i*, *o*, or *u*).

> There is **an** elephant.

> There is **an** animal.

Use *a* before words that do not start with a vowel
sound.

> There is **a** dolphin.

> There is **a** bear.

B   Complete the sentences. Circle the correct
answers.

1   There is **a** / **an** old photo.

2   This is **a** / **an** famous building.

3   This is **a** / **an** beautiful city.

4   There is **a** / **an** island near here.

C   Look at the pictures. Write sentences.

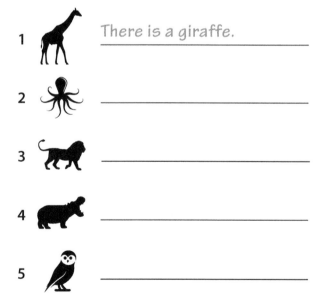

1   There is a giraffe. _____

2   _____

3   _____

4   _____

5   _____

4

THIS IS MY **FAMILY**

PREVIEW

A **Label the photo above.** Use the words in the box.

> mother   father   brother   sister   ~~me~~

1 _____me_____   2 _____   3 _____   4 _____   5 _____

B **Complete the diagram.** Use the words from **A** (**2–5**) and the words in the box.

> niece   grandparents
> daughter   parents
> nephew   son
> aunt   uncle
> cousin

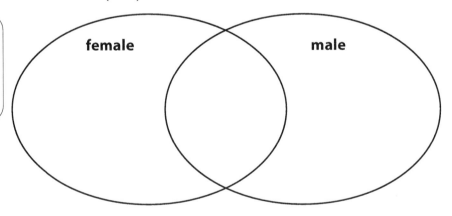

female   male

C **Complete the sentences.** Use the words from **B**.

1 Your mother's sister is your _____.

2 Your mother's brother is your _____.

LANGUAGE FOCUS

A Complete the conversation. Write the correct form of *have* or *do*.

Steve: Rosa, who's that in the photo?

Rosa: That's my uncle. My dad
¹ _____ three brothers.

Steve: Really? My dad ² _____
any brothers or sisters.

Rosa: So, ³ _____ your mom
have any brothers or sisters? My
mom has three sisters.

Steve: Cool! My mom has one brother.
⁴ _____ you have many
cousins?

Rosa: Yeah! I ⁵ _____ nine!

Steve: Really?

Rosa: Yeah. They are all girls. They ⁶ _____ any brothers!

Steve: Wow! I only ⁷ _____ one cousin called Carlos.

B Look at the photo. Complete the questions and answers.

1 Who are Ruth and Peter?
   <u>They are Jenny and Ann's parents</u> .

2 Does Jenny have a baby brother?
   _____ .

3 _____ ?
   No, Ann doesn't have any brothers.

4 _____ ?
   Yes, they have two daughters.

5 Does Jenny have any sisters?
   _____ .

C Match. Join the two parts of the conversation.

1 Does she have any cousins? ○   ○ **a** Yes. I have one brother.

2 Do they have any uncles? ○   ○ **b** Yeah, she has three cousins.

3 Do you have a brother? ○   ○ **c** No, he doesn't.

4 Do you have any sisters? ○   ○ **d** No, they don't.

5 Does he have any brothers? ○   ○ **e** No, I don't have any sisters.

Dan — Paola

Beth — Massimo   Matteo   Marco — Franca

Andre   Rebecca   Carol   ME

PEOPLE IN MY FAMILY

A Look at the family tree. Answer the questions.

1 Who's your aunt? _____

2 Who are your cousins? _____

3 Who's your grandmother? _____

4 Who are your uncles? _____

5 Who is your dad's niece? _____

6 Who's your mom's nephew? _____

B Complete each sentence with two or three words. Use information from the family tree.

1 My grandparents _____ sons.

2 Massimo _____ children.

3 Dan and Paola _____ grandchildren.

4 Matteo _____ sisters.

READING

A **Skim the article.** What is it about?

   a grandparents   **b** family   **c** sisters

MY FAMILY

This is Sydney Stewart. Her favorite singer is Ariana Grande. Sydney is a singer, too.

Sydney lives with her family in Los Angeles. It's in California, in the United States. Ariana
5 Grande lives in the Los Angeles area, too.

Sydney's father, Frank, is 44 years old. Frank has two sisters. Amelia is 38 and has a daughter. They live in New York. Frank's other sister, Angelina, is 42. She doesn't have
10 any children.

Sydney has a brother, Jerry. He really likes baseball. His favorite team is the L.A. Dodgers. He likes the L.A. Lakers basketball team and the L.A. Rams football team, too.

B   **EXAM PRACTICE**   **Answer the questions about _My Family_.**

  1   MAIN IDEA   What's another title for this article?

    a Frank's Sisters   **b** Jerry and His Friends   **c** Sydney and Her Family

  2   REFERENCE   The word _It's_ in line 4 refers to _____.

    a Sydney's house   **b** Los Angeles   **c** Ariana Grande's house

  3   DETAIL   Who is NOT in Sydney's immediate family?

    a Frank   **b** Amelia   **c** Jerry

  4   INFERENCE   According to the article, how many cousins does Sydney have?

    a one   **b** two   **c** three

  5   DETAIL   Jerry's favorite baseball team is _____.

    a the L.A. Rams   **b** the L.A. Lakers   **c** the L.A. Dodgers

C **Answer the questions.**

  1 Who's in your immediate family? _____

  2 How many cousins are there in your extended family? _____

  3 What countries do your aunts and uncles live in? _____

VOCABULARY

A Match. Join the two parts of the sentences.

1 My mom likes to add   ○   ○   **a**   is to make a cake together.

2 I love winter,   ○   ○   **b**   our family traditions.

3 My grandmother continues   ○   ○   **c**   popular with the local people.

4 That small store is   ○   ○   **d**   apple to her salads.

5 My family's birthday tradition   ○   ○   **e**   enjoys baseball.

6 My grandfather   ○   ○   **f**   especially the cold!

B Complete the sentences. Use the words in the box.

> great-grandmother   great-aunt   great-grandfather   great-uncle

1 Your grandmother's brother is your _____.

2 Your mother's grandfather is your _____.

3 Your father's grandmother is your _____.

4 Your grandfather's sister is your _____.

A family in Greece shares a meal.

WRITING

WRITING TIP Using apostrophes

Use apostrophes (') to show possession and to make contractions. Contractions are the short form of two words.

A Read the information.

Possession: show relationships

> That is Sarah**'s** book, and that is Paul**'s** pencil.

> Frank is Sydney**'s** father.

Contractions combine a subject and verb. They also combine a verb and *not*.

> **He is** a student. = **He's** a student.

> She **does not** have any children. = She **doesn't** have any children.

B Read the sentences. Write the names to complete the family tree.

1 Sue's husband is Bob.

2 My name is Jessie.

3 My uncle is Steve.

4 Steve's sister is Ruth.

5 Jack's wife is Ruth.

6 Leah is my sister.

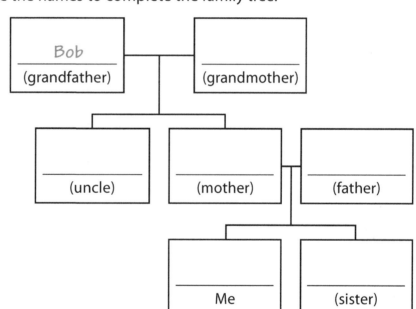

C Write. Use the family tree in **The Real World** section. Write sentences about the family. Use an apostrophe for both possession and contractions.

1 _____

2 _____

3 _____

4 _____

5 _____

6 _____

I LIKE **FRUIT!**

PREVIEW

A **Circle the hidden words.** Use the pictures to help you.

A	W	A	T	E	R	M	E	L	O	N
M	E	P	A	P	E	B	G	I	P	O
I	E	P	I	N	E	A	P	P	L	E
L	L	L	O	R	A	N	G	E	S	C
K	M	E	A	T	B	A	N	F	M	H
C	H	I	C	K	E	N	F	I	S	E
H	O	R	A	N	E	A	E	S	Z	R
E	S	A	N	D	W	I	C	H	V	R
Y	E	A	H	S	O	U	P	E	P	Y

B **Complete the chart.** Use the words from **A**.

Countable Nouns	Uncountable Nouns
apple	meat

C   Write. List the kinds of fruit in **A**.

_____

LANGUAGE FOCUS

A   Look at the chart. What do the students like to eat? Complete the sentences.

	Junko	Henry	Lara
cherries	☺	☺	☹
vegetables	☺	☺	☺
milk	☹	☹	☺

1 Junko and Henry _____ like _____ cherries.

2 Lara _____ vegetables.

3 Lara _____ cherries.

4 Two people _____ milk.

5 Three people _____ vegetables.

6 Junko: "I _____ milk, but I _____ vegetables."

B   Complete the conversations. Circle the correct answers.

1 A: Do you **like / likes** popcorn?

   B: Yes, I do.

2 A: I really like soup. Do you?

   B: No, I **do / don't**.

3 A: **Does / Don't** Ying like soda?

   B: No, she doesn't.

4 A: Does Alan like chicken?

   B: Yes, he **do / does**.

5 A: **Do / Does** they like meat?

   B: Yes, they do.

6 A: Hey, Maria, do you like vegetables?

   B: Yes, I **do / does**.

C   Complete the conversation. Put the words in the correct order to make questions and sentences.

Dylan: have / I'm / lunch / hungry! / Let's

May: you / like / meat / Do

Dylan: I / but / don't, / like / I / vegetables / No,

May: you / like / Do / rice

Dylan: do. / I / really / I / like / it / Yes,

May: have / Let's / vegetables / rice and

1 I'm hungry! Let's have lunch .

2 _____ ?

3 _____ .

4 _____ ?

5 _____ .

6 _____ .

THE REAL WORLD

A **Read the article.** Match the lunches with the countries.

| India | South Korea | France |

1 _____ 2 _____ 3 _____

What do you eat for lunch at school? School lunches are different in different countries.

This is a lunch in South Korea. All of the students eat the same lunch at the same time. There's usually soup and rice with every lunch. There's also sometimes meat, kimchi, and vegetables.

In France, students eat bread, but they don't have sandwiches. The French students also eat meat, salad, and cheese.

Here's a school lunch from India. This lunch has bread, too. It also has curry and rice.

B **Complete the chart.** Check (✓) the food items from each country.

	South Korea	France	India
bread			
curry			
meat			
rice			
soup			
vegetables			
cheese			

READING

A Look at the photo. What do you think the article is about?

a   a clothes market

b   a food market

c   a shoe market

FLOATING MARKETS

People from many countries go to Thailand. Some people visit the floating markets. The floating markets are boats on water. The boats have food. They have many other things, too.

5   Some of the markets are near Bangkok, the capital city of Thailand. There are many boats, and people from around the world go on them.

Look at the photo. What do you see? There are bananas, apples, and coconuts. Some boats have fruits like dragon
10 fruit and oranges. Other boats have vegetables and flowers. There are boats with fish and meat, too. It all looks delicious!

A market seller in Ratchaburi, Thailand

B   EXAM PRACTICE   Answer the questions about *Floating Markets*.

1   MAIN IDEA   What's another title for this article?

a   The Food Boats   b   Favorite Fruit   c   Lunch in Thailand

2   VOCABULARY   The word *floating* in line 2 means _____ .

a   on the water   b   next to the water   c   under the water

3   DETAIL   According to the article, _____ often go on the boats.

a   photographers   b   gardeners   c   tourists

4   INFERENCE   According to the article, the floating markets are _____ .

a   quiet   b   popular   c   small

5   DETAIL   The writer thinks the food at the floating market looks _____ .

a   beautiful   b   colorful   c   tasty

C   Answer the questions.

1   Is there a market like this in your country? _____

2   Which fresh food do you buy at a market? _____

VOCABULARY

A Complete the sentences. Circle the correct answers.

1 Carl Warner's foodscapes look **real** / **dangerous**. They are amazing!

2 This dessert is **the same as** / **made of** chocolate.

3 My dad **shapes** / **builds** houses.

4 That restaurant's food is very **fresh** / **old**.

5 A **landscape** / **camouflage** shows a city or a natural place.

B Match. Join each kind of food to an example.

1 fresh food   ○   ○ **a** food your family cooks

2 homemade food ○   ○ **b** burgers and pizza

3 fast food   ○   ○ **c** meat and vegetables from the market

C Complete the sentences. Use the words from **B**.

1 I like buying fruit from markets with _____ food.

2 We prefer _____ food to eating out at restaurants.

3 There is too much _____ food at the school cafeteria, like chicken nuggets and fries.

A family in Singapore enjoys a meal together.

WRITING

WRITING TIP Using commas in lists

Use commas (**,**) to separate words in lists.

A Read the information.

Example:

Fried rice is made from …
1 eggs   2 meat   3 vegetables   4 rice

You can write a sentence using commas:

Fried rice is made from eggs**,** meat**,** vegetables**,** and rice.

B Look at the text below. What is it?

a a website   b a school notebook   c a page from a book

Message Board

What food do you like?

Posted: 6:55 p.m. by May

Hi. My name is May. I like fast food. I like pizza and burgers. I like chips and chocolate, too. I don't like rice.

Posted: 6:59 p.m. by Jack

Hello. I'm Jack. I'm really into fruit! I love cherries, watermelons, and pineapples. I don't like noodles.

Posted: 7:05 p.m. by David

My name is David. I like homemade food, especially dishes with rice, meat, or cheese. I don't like bread.

C Read the messages in B. Write a message about the food you like.

_____

_____

_____

_____

_____

6 WHAT TIME DOES CLASS START?

PREVIEW

A **Match.** Join the pictures to the correct phrases.

1 ○   ○ **a** get up

2 ○   ○ **b** do homework

3 ○   ○ **c** go to school

4 ○   ○ **d** have dinner

5 ○   ○ **e** go to bed

6 ○   ○ **f** go home

B **Look at the times.** Write the times in numbers.

1 eight fifteen ___8:15___

2 seven o'clock _____

3 eleven thirty _____

4 one thirty _____

5 twelve fifteen _____

6 five forty-five _____

C **Complete the diagram.** Use the words in the box.

~~usually~~   sometimes   always   often   never

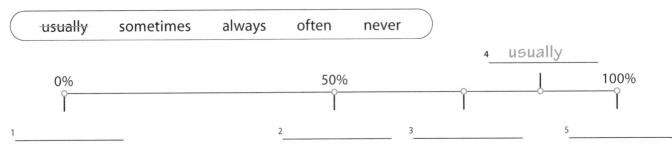

LANGUAGE FOCUS

A Complete the sentences and questions. Circle the correct answers.

1 When **do / does** he have table tennis practice?

2 What time **do / does** you watch TV?

3 What time do they **eat / eats** lunch?

4 They **goes / go** to school every day.

5 When does class **start / starts**?

6 I **has / have** breakfast at 6:15.

B Look at the chart. Complete the sentences.

RACHEL'S SCHEDULE					
	MONDAY	**TUESDAY**	**WEDNESDAY**	**THURSDAY**	**FRIDAY**
get up	6:00	6:30	6:00	6:00	6:00
go to school	7:00	7:15	7:00	6:30	7:30
go home	5:00	5:00	5:00	5:00	5:00
have dinner	7:00	7:30	6:45	7:00	7:45
do homework	8:00	8:00	8:00	8:30	9:00
go to bed	10:30	10:45	10:45	11:15	11:45

1 Rachel usually _____ *gets up* _____ at 6:00.

2 She always _____ at 5:00.

3 She never _____ dinner at 6:30.

4 Rachel often _____ at 8 o'clock.

5 Sometimes she _____ at 10:45.

C Write sentences about your schedule. Use the words in the box.

(~~usually~~   sometimes   always   often   never)

1 *I usually do my homework in the library.* _____

2 _____

3 _____

4 _____

5 _____

Students from Atlanta build a
Ford Daytona '65 Coupe.

A **Skim the article.** What do you think it is about?

a transportation   b learning   c schools

A Special Classroom

Barrington Irving is a pilot. He thinks education is important. He wants students to see how science, technology, art, and math work together. He started Experience Aviation so students can do interesting projects.

In one project, more than 50 students in Atlanta build a car from 1965— a Ford Daytona Coupe. They use about 1,000 car pieces. It takes 18 weeks to finish the car. The project is exciting for students. They think building a fast, beautiful car is awesome. Many students think they want to work in technology and science in the future.

B **Complete the chart.** Use information from *A Special Classroom*.

Name of organization	
Founder of organization	
Purpose of project	
Number of students	
Amount of materials used	
Time taken	

READING

A Skim the letter. Check (✓) the things Petra talks about.

☐ school subjects   ☐ weekend activities   ☐ after school activities   ☐ her favorite food

	Dear Trisha,
	My name's Petra. Here's some information about me.
	On weekdays, I get up at 6:30. On the weekends, I never get up at 6:30. That's
	too early! I get up at 9 o'clock. What time do you get up on school days?
5	I usually go to school at 8:30. I study math, history, and English in the
	mornings. We always have lunch at 12 o'clock. Lunch is 45 minutes.
	My schedule changes every afternoon. I have geography on Mondays and PE on
	Fridays. I study art on Tuesdays and music on Thursdays. I have science on
	Wednesdays. That's my favorite subject! What's your favorite subject?
10	I finish school at 3:30, and then I go home. At home, I do my homework, have
	dinner, watch TV, and then go to bed. What do you do after school?
	Hope to hear from you very soon!
	Petra

B **EXAM PRACTICE** **Answer the questions about Petra's letter.**

1 MAIN IDEA What's the article about?

   a Petra's school day   **b** Petra's hobbies   **c** Petra's family

2 DETAIL How many classes does Petra have in the morning?

   a 2   **b** 3   **c** 4

3 INFERENCE What time does Petra finish lunch?

   a 12:10   **b** 12:35   **c** 12:45

4 REFERENCE *That's* in line 9 refers to _____ .

   a English   **b** art   **c** science

5 VOCABULARY The phrase *very soon* means about _____ .

   a one week   **b** four months   **c** one year

C **Complete the schedule.** Write the activities that Petra does at the different times.

	Monday	Tuesday	Wednesday	Thursday	Friday	Saturday	Sunday
6:30 a.m.	gets up						
8:30 a.m.							
9:00 a.m.							
12 p.m.							
12:45 p.m.				studies music	has PE		
3:30 p.m.							

VOCABULARY

A **Complete the sentences and questions.** Use the words in the box.

early   get married   dream   enough   finish   history

1 What time do you usually _____ school?

2 Do you have _____ time to do your homework and watch TV?

3 I want to _____ in that amazing building in my town.

4 My _____ is to be a singer. I love music!

5 Who is your favorite person from _____ ?

6 On weekdays, I get up _____ for school.

B **Complete the chart.** Write about schools in your country and the subjects you learn there.

EDUCATION HISTORY

Level	Subjects
Kindergarten	

WRITING

WRITING TIP **Writing a letter**

We write informal letters to friends and family. The letters have a general format.

A Read the information.

opening greeting ⟶	Dear Petra,
thank Petra for her letter ⟶	Thank you for the letter.
about you ⟶	My name is
about your daily schedule ⟶	
about your school subjects ⟶	
question(s) for Petra ⟶	
closing ⟶	Best wishes,
your name ⟶	

B Plan your letter. Answer these questions.

1 What is your daily schedule? _____

_____

_____

2 What subjects do you study at school? _____

_____

3 What information do you want to learn about Petra? _____

_____

C Write a letter. Use your answers from part **B**, ideas from other parts of the unit, and your own ideas to write a letter to Petra.

7 CAN ELEPHANTS SWIM?

PREVIEW

A **Label the pictures.** Use the words in the box.

> jump   drums   fly   climb   piano   swim   dance   tool

1 _____

2 _____

3 _____

4 _____

5 _____

6 _____

7 _____

8 _____

B **Complete the chart.** Use the words from **A**.

Actions	Things

C **Complete the phrases.** Circle the correct answers.

1 climb **a mountain / the sea**

2 use **a guitar / a tool**

3 fly **in the sky / on a mountain**

4 play **a tool / the drums**

LANGUAGE FOCUS

A **Complete the conversation.**

Ana: Kelly, this is my friend, Jack. He's really into sports.

He [1] _____can_____ play baseball and soccer.

Kelly: Hi, Jack, I'm Kelly. [2] _____ you play tennis?

Jack: Hi, Kelly. No, I [3] _____ .

Kelly: What languages [4] _____ you speak?

Jack: I [5] _____ speak Portuguese and English.

Ana: Wow! Today is music class. Can you [6] _____ the drums, Jack?

Jack: Yes, I [7] _____ .

Kelly: Great, do you want to play in our band?

Jack: Yeah!

B **Complete the chart with your own answers.** Then complete the questions and answers.

	Paula	Lucas	You
sing	✓	✓	
dance	X	X	
play the keyboard	X	✓	

1 Can Lucas play the keyboard? _____Yes, he can_____ .

2 Can Paula dance? _____ .

3 What can Paula and Lucas do? _____ .

4 _____ play the keyboard? No, she can't.

5 Can you _____ ? _____ .

6 What _____ ? I can _____ .

C **Match.** Join the two parts of the conversation.

1 What's that?   ○   ○ **a** I can sing. I sing in a band.

2 Can you draw?   ○   ○ **b** It's my painting.

3 What can you do?   ○   ○ **c** Yeah. I really like to draw animals.

4 Can you play the drums? ○   ○ **d** No, I'm not good at music.

THE REAL WORLD

A New Caledonian crow carries a stick.

A Predict. Can New Caledonian crows plan? _____

Crow Intelligence

Can New Caledonian crows solve a puzzle? Scientists want to find out. They make a puzzle. The crows can get food, but only by completing three steps.

The scientists put a small box on a table. This is the puzzle. The scientists don't show the crows the steps to find the food. The crows need to solve the puzzle to get the food. First, the crows take a branch. Second, the crows use the branch to move a rock. For the third step, the crows use the rock to open a door. Then they get some food.

Not all of the crows can do this the first time they see the puzzle, but some can! The crows understand each step and can use tools to get food. The scientists are amazed. The crows can plan their actions!

B Read the article. Circle the correct answers.

1 The scientists make the puzzle difficult by _____.

  a watching the crows   **b** hiding each step   **c** giving food

2 The third step is to _____.

  a get a branch   **b** move a rock   **c** open a door

3 The scientists probably put the food _____.

  a behind the door   **b** under the rock   **c** in front of the box

4 _____ of the crows solve the puzzle the first time.

  a All   **b** Some   **c** None

READING

A **Skim the article.** What's special about Dema and Nia?

  a They're friends.
     b They like the same food.
     c They're the same age.

DEMA AND NIA

This is Dema and his good friend, Nia.

Dema is a Sumatran tiger. He's black and orange. Nia is orange, too, but she isn't a tiger. She's a Sumatran orangutan.

There aren't many Sumatran tigers and orangutans now. They live in the Taman Safari Zoo in Indonesia. Tigers and orangutans aren't usually friends, but Dema and Nia are babies. They are friends, and they are happy together.

Tigers

Tigers are smart.

They can climb trees and swim.

They eat meat.

They can eat 27 kilograms of meat in one day.

They usually eat 5 kilograms of meat in one meal.

Orangutans

In Malay, *orangutan* means "person of the forest."

Orangutans are very smart.

They can climb trees.

They are usually in trees—90 percent of the time.

They often eat fruit and the leaves of trees.

B   **EXAM PRACTICE**   **Read the article.** Circle **T** for True, **F** for False, or **NG** for Not Given.

1	Nia and Dema can communicate with each other.	T	F	NG
2	They live in a zoo in Australia.	T	F	NG
3	Orangutans spend 10 percent of their time eating.	T	F	NG
4	Tigers can eat 27 kilograms of meat in one day.	T	F	NG

C **Complete the diagram.** Write the descriptions (**a–f**) .

  a ~~are orange~~

  b are smart

  c eat fruit

  d can swim

  e can climb trees

  f are usually in trees

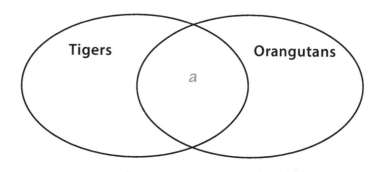

VOCABULARY

A Complete the sentences. Use the words in the box.

> smart   understand   zoo   points   hot   communicate

1 Kanzi _____ at pictures on a computer to talk to people.

2 Some animals live in a(n) _____ .

3 Be careful! The soup is _____ .

4 Many people say dogs are _____ animals.

5 I use social media to _____ with people in other countries.

6 Over 1.5 billion people around the world can _____ English.

B Match. Join the two parts of the conversation.

1 It's cold.   ○   ○   **a** Let's make dinner.

2 I want to talk to my grandmother. ○   ○   **b** Let's make plans.

3 I'm hungry.   ○   ○   **c** Let's make a fire.

4 I want to go to Brazil.   ○   ○   **d** Let's make a call.

C Complete the sentences. Use the words from **B**.

1 When we go camping, we usually make a _____ to keep ourselves warm.

2 Are you busy on Saturday? Let's make _____ to see a movie or go shopping.

3 It's mom's birthday today. Let's make _____ for her as a surprise.

4 I wonder how Tom is. Let's make a _____ and find out.

WRITING

WRITING TIP **Using commas in sentences**

Commas (,) are often used in sentences to show pauses in speech.

A Read the information.

Can Lucy paint? Yes, she can.

short pause when talking

Can Peter dance? No, he can't.

short pause

B Complete the diagram. What can your friends do? Write the names of five friends in the correct sections.

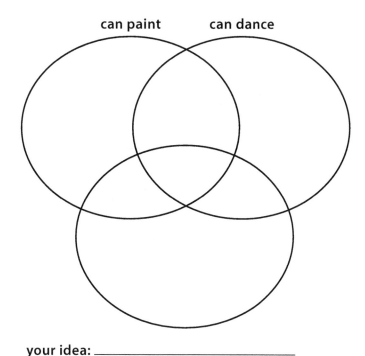

can paint   can dance

your idea: _____

C Write. Write questions and answers about what your friends can and can't do. Use commas in the sentences.

1 _____

2 _____

3 _____

4 _____

5 _____

8

HOW MUCH IS THAT T-SHIRT?

PREVIEW

A Complete the puzzle. Use the chart.

1	2	3	4	5	6	7	8	9	10	11	12	13	14	15	16	17	18
a	b	c	d	e	g	h	i	j	k	l	n	o	p	r	s	t	w

1 <u>h</u> <u>a</u> <u>t</u>
    7   17

2 ___ ___ ___ ___ ___
    16   7   15

3 ___ ___ ___ ___
       7   13

4 ___ ___ ___ ___ ___
    17   7   8

5 ___ ___ ___ ___ ___
    18   11   5

6 ___ ___ ___ ___ ___ ___ ___
    2   3   10   1

B Label the pictures. Use the words from **A**.

1 _____ 2 _____ 3 _____

4 _____ 5 _____ 6 _____

LANGUAGE FOCUS

A Complete the conversations. Circle the correct answers.

1 Buyer: **I'd like** / **I'd** that T-shirt, please.

   Seller: Here you are.

2 Buyer: Excuse me. I'd **like to see** / **like to** those shoes.

   Seller: Here you go.

3 Seller: Would you like **see** / **to see** these sneakers?

   Buyer: No, thanks. **I'd** / **I'm** like those ones, please.

4 Seller: How **much** / **like** is that wallet?

   Buyer: **It's** / **They're** only $15.

B Complete the conversations.

1 Seller: Would you ¹ _____ to see this pink T-shirt?

   Buyer: No, thanks. ² _____ like the blue one, please. How much ³ _____ it?

   Seller: ⁴ _____ only $9.

2 Buyer: Excuse me. How much ⁵ _____ those shoes?

   Seller: ⁶ _____ $125.

   Buyer: Hmmm, that's too expensive. ⁷ _____ much are those sneakers?

   Seller: They're $75. ⁸ _____ you like to see them?

   Buyer: Yes, please.

C Read the ads. Complete the questions and answers.

THE DAILY HERALD EDITION CLASSIFIEDS

FOR SALE

Old sweatshirts. $8 for one.
Call George 090-7555-1234.

FOR SALE

One red T-shirt for $5. It's from Indonesia.
Email Lisa: lisa@mail.com

FOR SALE

New sneakers from Los Angeles,
the United States. $20.
Contact Karen: karen.sneakers@mail.com

1 A: How much are the sweatshirts?

   B: _____They're $ 8_____ .

2 A: _____ ?

   B: It's $5.

3 A: What color is that T-shirt?

   B: _____ .

4 A: _____ ?

   B: They're $20.

5 A: _____ see

   these _____ ?

   They're only $8.

   B: Yes, please.

THE REAL WORLD

Shoppers at a market in India

A **Complete the summary.** Circle the correct answers.

Haggling is a conversation between [1] **a buyer and a seller** / **two sellers**. The buyer wants to get something for a(n) [2] **expensive** / **cheap** price. The buyer and seller usually agree on a price [3] **from the beginning** / **after discussing more than one price**.

B **Complete the conversation.** Use the prices in the box.

> $10 $15 $17 $20

Buyer: Excuse me. Can I see that, please?

Seller: Sure, here you go.

Buyer: How much is it?

Seller: It's [1] _____ .

Buyer: That's too expensive. How about [2] _____ ?

Seller: That's too cheap. I can sell it for [3] _____ .

Buyer: That's still too expensive.

Seller: You can have it for [4] _____ .

Buyer: OK, I'd like it, please.

READING

A Scan the article. Write three activities people can do at the mall.

_____

SHOP AND SWIM!

West Edmonton Mall is a really big mall in Canada. There are over 800 stores in the mall. Customers can buy clothes, shoes, wallets, and watches—it sells many things. There are lots of things to do at
5 the mall, too. You can watch a movie, go ice skating, eat—and shop!

West Edmonton Mall has an underground aquarium, with over 100 different kinds of fish, turtles, and other sea animals. And there's also an
10 indoor waterpark in the mall. You can swim in the pool and play in the waterpark. West Edmonton Mall is really cool!

B EXAM PRACTICE Answer the questions about _Shop and Swim!_

1 MAIN IDEA What's another title for the article?

   a An Awesome Mall   **b** Food Shops   **c** Haggling at the Market

2 DETAIL You can _____ in West Edmonton Mall.

   a take a dance class   **b** eat   **c** play basketball

3 INFERENCE What animals can you probably NOT see in the mall?

   a seals   **b** elephants   **c** sharks

4 DETAIL There is a waterpark _____ the mall.

   a under   **b** near   **c** in

5 INFERENCE West Edmonton Mall is special because regular malls don't usually _____ .

   a have stores underground   **b** open for 24 hours   **c** have a waterpark

C Answer the questions.

1 Would you like to go to this shopping mall?

_____

2 Is there a shopping mall like this in your city?

_____

VOCABULARY

A **Complete the sentences and questions.** Circle the correct answers.

1 **A:** Can I see that red shirt, please?

   B: Here you go.

   A: It's too big for me. Sorry, can I have the white one **instead** / **only**?

2 Your paintings are beautiful! You are very **quiet** / **creative**.

3 **Customers** / **Businesses** love that Chinese restaurant.

4 Most college students have cellphones. They are very **common** / **strong**.

5 There's a new restaurant in town. Let's go and **try** / **pay** the food.

6 I want to buy this. Can I **finish** / **pay** with an app?

B **Complete the sentences.** Use the words in the box.

> wake up   look up   give up

1 I usually _____ at 6:45.

2 Don't _____ ! You can do it!

3 I don't understand how this app works. I need to _____ some information on the internet.

WRITING

WRITING TIP **Informal words**

In English, there is formal and informal writing, and sometimes the words we use are different.

A Read the information.

Emails, text messages, and blogs are usually informal.

FORMAL	INFORMAL
Hello. / Good-bye.	Hi. / Bye.
There is a very interesting market.	There's a really cool market.
That restaurant is not near the city.	That restaurant is in the middle of nowhere.
I really like to play computer games.	I'm into computer games.

B Plan your text message. Your friend is visiting your city next week. Choose a mall or market in your city to take your friend to. Write notes about it.

1 What's the place like? Is it big or small?

_____

2 What's interesting about this place?

_____

3 What does it have there?

_____

4 What can people do there?

_____

C Write a text message to your friend. Describe the mall or market in your city.

_____

_____

_____

_____

_____

_____

_____

9

WHAT ARE YOU DOING?

PREVIEW

A   Match. Join each word or phrase to its correct picture.

1   checking email   ○   ○ a   📷

2   chatting   ○   ○ b   ✉

3   calling a friend   ○   ○ c   📱💬

4   playing a game   ○   ○ d   📞

5   texting   ○   ○ e   💬👥

6   taking a photo   ○   ○ f   🎮

B   Complete the sentences. Circle the correct answers.

1   Many people use a computer to **chat** / **check** email.

2   I often **chat** / **take** with friends while I eat lunch.

3   You can **text** / **call** your family short messages from your phone.

4   You can **text** / **play** games on your laptop with people from around the world.

5   Nowadays you can **check** / **call** friends using many different apps.

6   Many people use their phones to **take** / **play** pictures.

LANGUAGE FOCUS

A **Complete the conversations.** Circle the correct answers.

1 Rafael: What are you **do** / **doing**?

   Alicia: **I'm** / **I** watching a movie.

2 Gilles: Are they **play** / **playing** video games?

   Marco: Yes, they **are** / **is**.

3 Dolores: Who **is** / **are** you texting?

   Wei: I'm **text** / **texting** my friend.

B **Correct one mistake in each sentence or question.**

1 Julie: Who are you text, Manuela?

   Manuela: I texting my mom.

2 David: Hey, Mark. What is you doing?

   Mark: I'm play games with my friend
               in Singapore.

3 Anna: Natalie, are Dana listening to music?

   Natalie: Yes, she are.

4 Matteo: Is your brothers watching a movie now?

   Jing: No, they are. They're playing
               basketball.

C **Look at the picture.** Complete the questions and answers.

1 Are Natalie and David using a computer? _____ .

2 _____ ? He's reading a book.

3 Is Manuela sitting in a library? _____ .

4 _____ ? He's listening to music.

5 What's Maria doing? _____ .

Corey Jaskolski explores an underwater cave in Mexico.

A Skim the article. What is it? Circle the correct answer.

a a web page   b a blog post   c an interview

ENGINEERS OF THE FUTURE

Interviewer: Hi Corey, you are an engineer. You explore amazing places around the world. Many young people want to be engineers. What should they study?

Corey: They need math and science, but they should also learn many different subjects. Information they learn from these subjects helps them think about problems in creative ways. I'm an engineer, but I make tools and machines for people in many other areas of science.

Interviewer: What else should young people do?

Corey: Ask lots of questions. That's the biggest part of being a good engineer. Asking questions helps them think of new ideas.

Interviewer: That's really helpful. Do you have any other advice for young people?

Corey: Go outside and take pictures. I do this a lot, and it's always interesting. You will see lots of cool things, and you can ask lots of questions!

B Read the article. Complete the summary. Use the words in the box.

> subjects   math   pictures   questions   science

Engineers work in many fields of [1] _____. Engineers mainly use science and

[2] _____ for their jobs, but they need to study many different [3] _____ in school. They

also need to think creatively about problems. Corey says it is important to ask [4] _____.

Taking [5] _____ helps people think about things in many different ways.

READING

A Look at the text. What is it?

a an email   **b** a blog post   **c** a text message

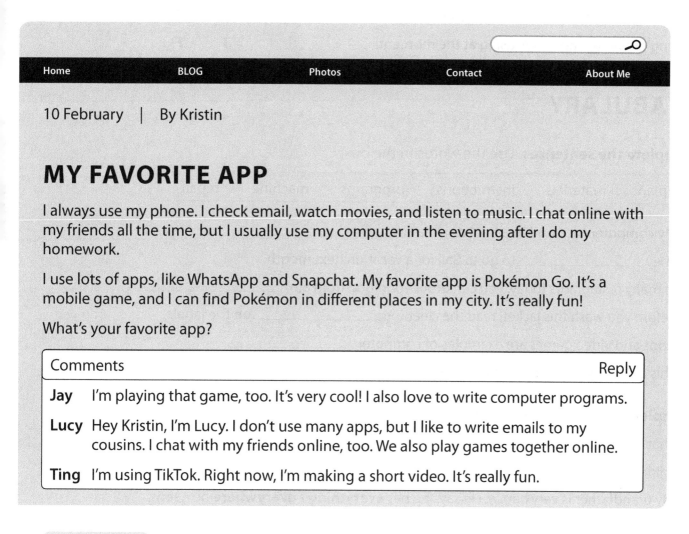

Home   BLOG   Photos   Contact   About Me

10 February | By Kristin

MY FAVORITE APP

I always use my phone. I check email, watch movies, and listen to music. I chat online with my friends all the time, but I usually use my computer in the evening after I do my homework.

I use lots of apps, like WhatsApp and Snapchat. My favorite app is Pokémon Go. It's a mobile game, and I can find Pokémon in different places in my city. It's really fun!

What's your favorite app?

Comments	Reply
Jay I'm playing that game, too. It's very cool! I also love to write computer programs.	
Lucy Hey Kristin, I'm Lucy. I don't use many apps, but I like to write emails to my cousins. I chat with my friends online, too. We also play games together online.	
Ting I'm using TikTok. Right now, I'm making a short video. It's really fun.	

B EXAM PRACTICE Answer the questions about *My Favorite App*.

1 MAIN IDEA Which of the following things does Kristin NOT do in her post?

   a describe her favorite app   **b** compare game apps   **c** list some apps she uses

2 DETAIL Kristin's favorite app is _____ .

   a Pokémon Go   **b** Snapchat   **c** WhatsApp

3 REFERENCE The word *We* in Lucy's comment refers to Lucy and _____ .

   a Kristin   **b** Jay   **c** her friends

4 INFERENCE TikTok is probably a _____ app.

   a travel   **b** health   **c** video sharing

5 DETAIL Who likes making short videos?

   a Ting   **b** Lucy   **c** Kristin

C **Read the article again.** Circle **T** for True or **F** for False.

1 Kristin uses her computer when she arrives home from school.   **T**   **F**

2 Kristin's favorite app is a mobile game.   **T**   **F**

3 Jay never plays mobile games.   **T**   **F**

4 Lucy likes to chat online with her friends.   **T**   **F**

5 Ting enjoys the app she's using at the moment.   **T**   **F**

VOCABULARY

A **Complete the sentences.** Use the words in the box.

> plan   materials   instructions   programs   machine   repair

1 My computer isn't working, but I don't know how to _____ it.

2 They _____ to go to Bali for a vacation next month.

3 In many restaurants today, you can order your food from a(n) _____.

4 Before you wash this jacket, read the cleaning _____ on the label.

5 Apps and video games are examples of computer _____.

6 This company makes bags from recycled _____ , such as plastic.

B **Complete the sentences.** Circle the correct answers.

1 That app is popular **everyone** / **everywhere**.

2 I didn't like the restaurant, but **everyone** / **everything** else liked it.

3 My grandfather is very happy. He says he has **everything** / **everywhere** he needs.

Customers order food from machines at a fast food restaurant in South Korea.

WRITING

WRITING TIP **Writing a blog post**

Writing a blog is a good way to practice English. You often use informal writing. You can communicate with people around the world.

A Read the information.

Give your blog post a title.
Name the topic.

Write about your topic.
Use informal language.

Ask other people questions.

> **My Favorite App**
>
> I use lots of apps, like WhatsApp and Snapchat. My favorite app is Pokémon Go. It's a mobile game, and I can find Pokémon in different places in my city. It's really fun!
>
> What's your favorite app?

B Write notes for your blog post. Answer the questions about your favorite activity.

What is the title of your blog post?	
What are the main topics for your blog post?	
What information can you include in your blog post?	
What question(s) can you ask other people?	

C Write a blog post about your favorite activity. Use your notes from **B**.

WHAT'S THE WEATHER LIKE?

PREVIEW

A Circle the hidden words. Use the pictures to help you.

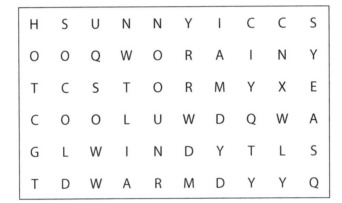

H	S	U	N	N	Y	I	C	C	S
O	O	Q	W	O	R	A	I	N	Y
T	C	S	T	O	R	M	Y	X	E
C	O	O	L	U	W	D	Q	W	A
G	L	W	I	N	D	Y	T	L	S
T	D	W	A	R	M	D	Y	Y	Q

B Complete the chart. Use the words from **A**.

Weather	Temperature
rainy	

C Write. Answer the questions about your city.

1 What's the weather like today? _____

2 Is it usually cold in the winter? _____

3 What's the weather like in the spring? _____

LANGUAGE FOCUS

A **Complete the conversation.** Write the correct words.

Matt: Hi, Ivan. [1] _____ the weather like in London?

Ivan: [2] _____ cold.

Matt: Really? [3] _____ cold is it?

Ivan: [4] _____ about 5 degrees and it's rainy.

Matt: Wow! [5] _____ it usually so cold in December?

Ivan: Yes, it [6] _____ .

B **Look at the chart.** Answer the questions.

CITY	WEATHER	TEMPERATURE (°C)
Los Angeles	☀	24°
Sacramento	🌧	13°
San Diego	⛈	21°
San Francisco	☁	14°

1 Is it rainy in Los Angeles? _____

2 What's the weather like in Sacramento? _____

3 What's the weather like in San Diego? _____

4 How hot is it in San Francisco? _____

C **Write the questions.**

1 What's the weather like in May?
_____

Well, in May it's usually warm, but sometimes it's cool.

2 _____

It's hot and dry today.

3 _____

It's about 30 degrees in the summer.

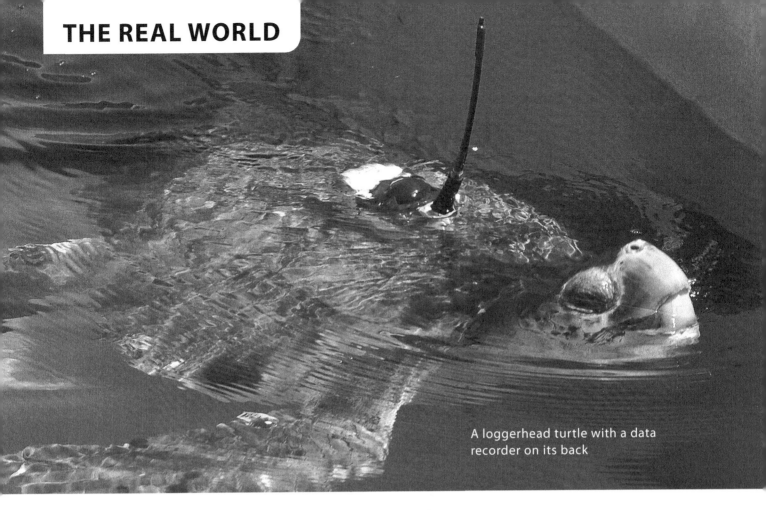

A loggerhead turtle with a data recorder on its back

THE REAL WORLD

A **Skim the article.** What do you think it is about? Circle the correct answer.

a ocean trash   b collecting information   c sick turtles

USING TECHNOLOGY TO LEARN

We can learn many things about an animal's world, but sometimes places deep in the ocean or high in the sky are difficult to see.

Katsufumi Sato is a scientist. He uses bio-logging—a new kind of science—to study different animals in their natural world. For example, he puts small data recorders on turtles. Then he lets the turtles go back into the wild.

Katsufumi finds out that green turtles are more likely than loggerhead turtles to eat dangerous things like plastic. This is important because plastic can cause turtles many problems. Turtles eat the plastic and then they aren't hungry enough to eat real food. Some scientists think green turtles don't understand that plastic is not food. They can use this information to find a way to help these turtles.

B **Read the article *Using Technology to Learn*.** Circle the correct answers.

1 Some scientists use **bio-logging / natural methods** to study animals deep in the ocean.

2 More **green turtles / loggerhead turtles** eat plastic.

3 The information from the turtles' data recorders helps scientists **study turtles' intelligence / study what turtles do in the ocean**.

READING

A Look at the photo. What do you think the article is about?

a snow   b storms   c fires

WILD WEATHER!

Hurricanes are unusual tropical storms. There are other
names for hurricanes—like cyclones and typhoons.
Hurricanes usually form in tropical areas and over
warm oceans.

A hurricane hits the
coast in Florida.

5 During a hurricane, there are often very strong winds,
storms, and heavy rain. The winds are very powerful—
sometimes over 250 kilometers an hour. In places like
Spain, Japan, and Canada—which are all in the Northern
Hemisphere—hurricane winds turn in one direction. In
10 places like Brazil and Australia—which are in the Southern
Hemisphere—they turn in the opposite direction. The
hurricane winds also make tall, dangerous waves in the ocean.

Hurricanes sometimes last for only a few hours, but other times they last for many days.
The center of the hurricane is called the eye. In the eye, the weather is usually very
15 different. It's often calm, sometimes with no rain. Sometimes you can even see the sky!

B Complete the word web. Use words from the article.

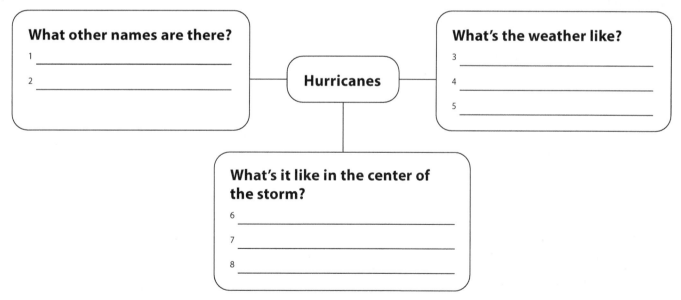

What other names are there?

1 _____

2 _____

Hurricanes

What's the weather like?

3 _____

4 _____

5 _____

**What's it like in the center of
the storm?**

6 _____

7 _____

8 _____

C EXAM PRACTICE Complete the summary. Circle the correct answers.

Tropical storms are usually in [1] **cool / warm** areas. Hurricanes probably do NOT have [2] **ice /
wind**. Tropical storms in the Southern Hemisphere turn in [3] **the same direction as /
the opposite direction to** storms in the Northern Hemisphere.

VOCABULARY

A Complete the sentences. Use the words in the box.

> launch   upload   temperature   views   record   projects

1 Science classes often have group _____ .

2 What's the _____ like in August? Is it more than 40°C?

3 There is a popular YouTube video with more than 6 billion _____ .

4 How many pictures do you _____ to social media every week?

5 Scientists _____ weather balloons into the sky every day.

6 Photos help us _____ events so people can remember them in the future.

B Rewrite the sentences. Use the phrasal verbs in the box.

> look out   find out   hang out   goes out

1 I like to spend time with my friends on the weekend.
   I like to hang out with my friends on the weekend.

2 My family usually goes to the beach on Sundays.

   _____

3 Be careful! That's dangerous.

   _____

4 I don't know, so I want to discover the answer.

   _____

A beach in
Calabria, Italy

WRITING

WRITING TIP **Using *but***

Use ***but*** to talk about two things that aren't the same.

A Read the information.

Use ***but*** to talk about one thing you like and one thing you don't like.

   I like sunny weather, **but** I don't like rainy weather.

Use a comma (,) before ***but*** when the two ideas are complete sentences.

   In the Northern Hemisphere, hurricane winds turn in one direction.

   In the Southern Hemisphere, they turn in the opposite direction.

   In the Northern Hemisphere, hurricane winds turn in one direction, **but** in the Southern Hemisphere, they turn in the opposite direction.

B Look at the chart. Add information about your city. Use real answers.

NAME	CITY	WEATHER	TEMPERATURE (°C)	
			TODAY	USUAL
David	London	sunny, very cold	2	9
Lisa	Sydney	hot, cloudy	30	24
You				

C Complete the conversation and circle the correct answers. Use the information in **B**.

Message Board

David: Hi, everyone. I have some homework. It's about the weather in other cities today. Can you help me?

You: Sure.

David: ¹Thanks. OK. I'm in _____ . It's _____ **and / but** _____ today.

Lisa: ²I'm in _____ . It's _____ **and / but** _____ today.

You: ³Uhh … well, I'm in _____ . It's _____ .

David: ⁴What's the temperature like today? Here, it's _____ **and / , but** usually it's _____ .

Lisa: ⁵Really? Here, it's _____ **and / , but** usually it's _____ .

You: ⁶_____ .

11 I WENT TO AUSTRALIA!

PREVIEW

A Complete the crossword puzzle. Use the pictures to help you.

Down

1

2

3

5

Across

4

6

B Complete the chart. Use the words from **A**.

PLACES	ACTIVITIES

LANGUAGE FOCUS

A Complete the conversation. Write the past forms of the verbs in parentheses.

Wei: Hi, Ethan. How [1]_____ (**is**) your vacation? Where did you go?

Ethan: Hi, Wei. I [2]_____ (**go**) to Xi'an in China. It [3]_____ (**is**) amazing! I had so much fun.

Wei: Wow! Xi'an! What [4]_____ (**do**) you do there?

Ethan: I [5]_____ (**walk**) on the city wall, and I [6]_____ (**eat**) a lot of delicious food.

Wei: Cool! [7]_____ (**do**) you see the terracotta soldiers?

Ethan: Of course! They [8]_____ (**are**) really amazing.

B Complete the conversation. Use the information in the calendar below.

AUGUST

MONDAY	TUESDAY	WEDNESDAY	THURSDAY	FRIDAY	SATURDAY	SUNDAY
		1	2	3	4 arrived in New Zealand Vacation	5 went to the beach
6	7 went hiking	8	9	10 visited an art museum	11 went sightseeing	12 went home

Sofia: Where did you go for vacation?

Ron: [1]_____ .

Sofia: [2]_____ ?

Ron: I went in August.

Sofia: What did you do?

Ron: Well, on the 5th, [3]_____ . Then two days later, [4]_____ .

Sofia: That sounds amazing! Did you go camping?

Ron: [5]_____ .

C Answer the questions. Use the information in the calendar.

1 What did Ron do on August 10th? _____ .

2 Did he go cycling? _____ .

3 When did he go home? _____ .

Alastair Humphreys on an adventure in Trosley County Park in the United Kingdom.

A **Look at the photo.** What do you think Alastair Humphreys did? _____

THE SKY'S THE LIMIT

Alastair Humphreys loves microadventures. He has them all the time. One time, Alastair went camping. He finished his work for the day. He got a group of friends together. They climbed a hill outside of town and watched the sunset. After that, they slept under the stars. In the morning, they enjoyed the sunrise, ran down the hill, and swam in the river. He even got back to work by 9 o'clock that morning!

Alastair wants everyone to know that they can have an adventure anywhere. So what's stopping you? Climb a hill. Watch the sun come up in the quiet of the morning. Enjoy the shooting stars. Dream it, and do it!

B **Read the article above.** Circle **T** for True or **F** for False.

1	Alastair often goes on microadventures.	**T**	**F**
2	Alastair's camping microadventure was probably expensive.	**T**	**F**
3	Alastair's camping microadventure took less than 24 hours.	**T**	**F**
4	Alastair wants all of us to try having a microadventure.	**T**	**F**

READING

A **Look at the text below.** What is it?

  a a letter   **b** a postcard   **c** a blog post

> Dear Chris,
>
> How are you? How was your vacation? During the summer, I went to an
> English-language summer school in Chicago in the United States. I stayed
> there for four weeks with an American host family. My American "parents"
> 5 were teachers. They have two sons and one daughter.
>
> In my class, there were students from all around the world. There was one
> student from China, two students from Thailand, and one student from Brazil.
> We had English class every weekday morning, Monday through Friday.
>
> After class in the afternoons, we visited many interesting places. We hiked
> 10 near the lake and swam in it, too. We also visited some museums. On the
> weekends, I hung out with my American family. We went to the mall, played
> tennis, and had barbecues in the park.
>
> I had a lot of fun! I hope I can go there again next year.
>
> Best wishes,
> 15 Yara

B   **EXAM PRACTICE**   **Answer the questions about Yara's trip.**

1   MAIN IDEA   Yara writes about _____ .

  a a hiking vacation   **b** a school trip   **c** a summer school

2   DETAIL   How long was Yara in the United States?

  a about a week   **b** about 30 days   **c** about two months

3 VOCABULARY The phrase *host family* in line 4 means _____.

  a Yara's immediate family   **b** the American family   **c** Yara's extended family
                                        Yara lived with

4 DETAIL What's one place Yara visited on weekday afternoons?

  a the museum   **b** the mall   **c** the park

5 REFERENCE The word *there* in line 13 refers to _____.

  a Brazil   **b** China   **c** the United States

C Answer the questions.

  1 What did you do last summer? _____

  2 Did you enjoy it? Why or why not? _____

VOCABULARY

A Match. Join the two parts of the sentences.

  1 My train arrived at   ○   ○ **a** I finally got 100% on my test.

  2 I started my journey   ○   ○ **b** so I am really tired.

  3 My family usually celebrates ○   ○ **c** in Brazil and finished in Peru.

  4 Deserts are always dry,   ○   ○ **d** 10 o'clock last night.

  5 I had four tests today,   ○   ○ **e** but not always hot.

  6 I'm really excited because   ○   ○ **f** my birthday at a restaurant.

B Complete the sentences. Circle the correct answers.

  1 The smartphone is a very **useful** / **colorful** invention.

  2 The market has all kinds of **helpful** / **colorful** fruit. It's beautiful!

  3 It's icy here so please be **useful** / **careful**.

  4 That book has a lot of **careful** / **helpful** ideas about how to study English.

A busy street in Paraty, Brazil

WRITING

WRITING TIP **Writing paragraphs**

A paragraph has one big idea.

A Read the information.

The first sentence usually has the main idea.

The other sentences have more information. They can also have examples.

Put an empty line between two paragraphs.

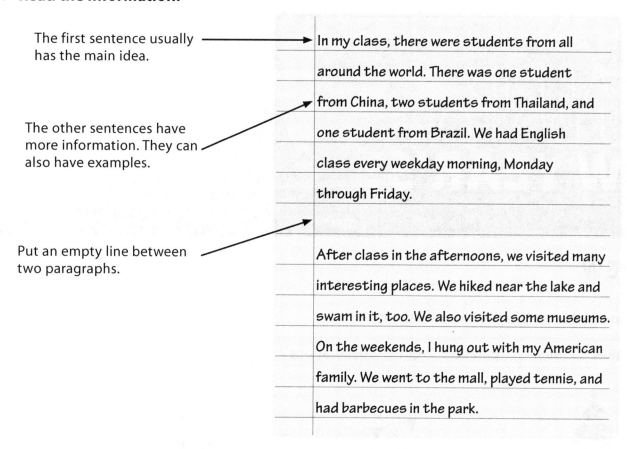

In my class, there were students from all around the world. There was one student from China, two students from Thailand, and one student from Brazil. We had English class every weekday morning, Monday through Friday.

After class in the afternoons, we visited many interesting places. We hiked near the lake and swam in it, too. We also visited some museums. On the weekends, I hung out with my American family. We went to the mall, played tennis, and had barbecues in the park.

B Complete the chart. You can make up ideas.

My Last Vacation	
Where did you go?	
When did you go?	
How many days was your vacation?	
What did you do?	1 2 3
Who did you go with?	
How was the vacation?	

C Write two short paragraphs about your last vacation. Use your notes from B.

12

WHAT DID YOU DO FOR NEW YEAR'S?

PREVIEW

A **Label the pictures.** Use the words in the box.

festival   meal   parade   gift   decorations   fireworks

1 festival

2 _____

3 _____

4 _____

5 _____

6 _____

B **Complete the phrases.** Circle the correct answers.

1 **played** / **prepared** a special meal

2 **watched** / **celebrated** a parade

3 **put** / **did** up decorations

4 **received** / **celebrated** a gift

5 **visited** / **watched** the fireworks

6 **put** / **went** to a festival

LANGUAGE FOCUS

A **Complete the conversations.** Circle the correct answers.

1 **Isabella:** Steve, when's your birthday?

  Steve: It's [1] **on / during** winter vacation.

  Max: So is mine! It's [2] **in / on** January 1st.

  Isabella: Wow! It's [3] **on / for** New Year's Day!

2 **Dana:** Where did you go [4] **in / for** July?

  Frank: I went to Iguazu Falls, between Brazil and Argentina. I was there [5] **for / in** five days. I got there [6] **on / in** July 15th.

  Dana: Really? I went there [7] **in / on** 2019. It was amazing!

B **Complete the sentences.** Use the simple past form of the verbs in parentheses.

1 I _____ (**spend**) three weeks in Africa last year.

2 They _____ (**have**) a birthday party on April 23rd.

3 On Saturday my family _____ (**put**) up decorations for the holidays.

4 I _____ (**eat**) amazing food during my winter vacation.

5 I _____ (**swim**) every day in July because it was so hot!

C **Complete the questions.** Use the information in the calendar below.

FEBRUARY

MONDAY	TUESDAY	WEDNESDAY	THURSDAY	FRIDAY	SATURDAY	SUNDAY
				1 Mom's birthday	2	3
4	5 School festival	6	7 Watch Chinese New Year fireworks.	8 No school. Visit grandma.	9	10

1 **A:** _____ What did you do for _____ Chinese New Year?

  B: I watched fireworks.

2 **A:** When _____?

  B: It's on February 1st.

3 **A:** Where _____?

  B: I went to school for the school festival.

THE REAL WORLD

Bread of the dead in
Oaxaca, Mexico

A Read the article. Circle the correct answers.

The Day of the Dead is a popular festival in Mexico. It goes on for three days at the end of October and beginning of November. During the event, people eat amazing food like *pan de muerto*—bread of the dead. The bread shops in Mexico make more than 400 types of *pan de muerto* during the festival. The bread is easy to make—just five ingredients, including eggs.

Some of the *pan de muerto* have bones and skulls on them. Others have arms, legs, and little faces called *caritas*. Some bakers start making the *caritas* as early as February! They need a lot of time to make thousands of small bread faces.

1 People probably celebrate the Day of the Dead on November **1st / 3rd**.

2 For the festival, people eat bread decorated with **colorful flowers / small faces**.

3 Some bakers start making the decorations for the bread **two / eight** months before the festival.

B Match. Join each description to its number.

1 number of types of *pan de muerto*   ○   ○ **a** 3

2 number of ingredients in *pan de muerto*   ○   ○ **b** 5

3 number of days people celebrate the Day of the Dead ○   ○ **c** 400

READING

A Scan the article. How many days does Diwali last?

a three   b four   c five

DIWALI

In October or November every year, Hindu people around the world celebrate the important festival of Diwali. Diwali—also called the "Festival of Lights"—lasts for
5 five days.

Hindu people usually do special things during Diwali. On the first day, they clean their homes. They also buy gold-colored things and things for the kitchen to bring
10 good fortune in the future. On the second day, some people make pictures with bright, colorful sand.

The third day is an important day in the festival. Families eat special food together.
15 They also watch fireworks.

A Diwali celebration in Jodhpur, India

The fourth day is the first day of the new year. People visit friends and extended family. They give gifts and wish them good luck. On the last day, brothers and sisters visit each other, and they eat amazing meals together.

Diwali is a happy time when people do a lot of fun things and eat a lot of great food.

B Read the article. Put the activities (**a–e**) in order from day 1 to day 5 of the festival.

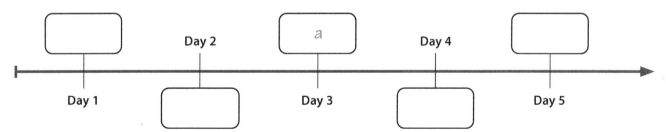

Day 1   Day 2   *a* Day 3   Day 4   Day 5

a watch fireworks

b clean the house

c make pictures with sand

d visit friends and relatives

e brothers and sisters visit each other

C **EXAM PRACTICE** **Answer the questions about *Diwali*.**

1 MAIN IDEA Diwali is a holiday for _____.

    a family   **b** young people   **c** women

2 INFERENCE Which of the following things are people likely to buy for Diwali?

    a books   **b** gold jewelry   **c** smartphones

3 DETAIL People usually spend _____ preparing their homes for Diwali.

    a two days   **b** five days   **c** a week

4 REFERENCE The word *they* in line 18 refers to _____.

    a friends   **b** brothers and sisters   **c** extended family

5 DETAIL What do people do on the last day?

    a visit a temple   **b** go shopping   **c** visit family

VOCABULARY

A **Complete the sentences.** Use the words in the box.

> last   hard   huge   sculptures   bright   competition

1 The ground gets really _____ in the winter when it's below zero.

2 There are many famous _____ in Europe, like *David* and *Venus de Milo*.

3 Our classes _____ for 45 minutes.

4 To celebrate the Dragon Boat Festival, different teams race against one another in a _____ .

5 This room has lots of windows so it's _____ even in the winter.

6 The sequoia trees in California are _____ . Some are about 75 meters tall.

B **Complete the sentences.** Circle the correct answers.

1 I forgot my wallet. Let's go **back** / **over** so I can get it.

2 I always go **over** / **down** my work many times to look for spelling mistakes.

3 The number of visitors go **through** / **down** in the winter.

4 Some people think going **back** / **through** difficult situations makes you stronger.

WRITING

WRITING TIP **ARTICLES**

Use *a*, *an*, and *the* with a single, countable noun. Don't use them with names.

A Read the information.

Use **a** for one countable thing when you don't know which one.

I gave my sister **a** present.

(We don't know which present.)

Use **the** for one countable thing that you know.

The present was in a huge box.

(Specific: We know *which* present "I gave my sister.")

Use **the** when there is only one in the world.

The Earth rotates around the sun.

(There is only one Earth.)

B Read the blog post. Underline the articles.

| Home | BLOG | Photos | Contact | About Me |

Hi! I'm from Munich, Germany. This is a photo from Oktoberfest. We celebrate this festival every year in September or October. Tourists from around the world come to celebrate, too. It's an amazing festival.

The festival started over 200 years ago. It lasts for about 16 days. During the festival, people sometimes wear beautiful costumes. It's an old tradition. They meet friends, family, and relatives. They eat special food. It's a fun day!

C Write a blog post about a festival.

LANGUAGE NOTES

UNIT 1 WHAT'S YOUR FAVORITE VIDEO GAME?

TALKING ABOUT FAVORITES (USING *WHAT*, *WHO*, AND POSSESSIVE ADJECTIVES)		
What's your favorite movie?	**My** / **Our** favorite movie **is** *Spider-Man*.	What's = What is
What's his favorite music app?	**His** favorite music app **is** Apple Music.	Who's = Who is
What's their favorite color?	**Their** favorite color **is** orange.	
Who's her favorite singer?	**Her** favorite singer **is** Bruno Mars.	

UNIT 2 THIS PLACE IS AMAZING!

DESCRIBING PLACES (USING *BE* AND ADJECTIVES)		
This place **is famous**. / The buildings **are amazing**. They**'re** very **new**. They**'re not old**. / They **aren't old**.		They're = They are They're not = They are not aren't = are not isn't = is not
Is the street **long**?	**Yes**, it **is**. **No**, it **isn't** / it**'s not**.	
Are the houses **big**?	**Yes**, they **are**. **No**, they **aren't** / they**'re not**.	

UNIT 3 WHERE'S THE LION?

TALKING ABOUT LOCATION OF THINGS (USING PREPOSITIONS)	
The bears are **near** the tree. The monkey is **behind** the frog.	
How many animals **are there**?	**There's** one animal. / **There are** twenty animals.
Where's the frog?	It's **on** / **under** / **next to** the rock.
Where are the monkeys?	They're **in front of** / **behind** the tree.
Is the lion **on** the rock?	Yes, it is. / No, it isn't.
Are the fish **in** the water?	Yes, they are. / No, they aren't.

UNIT 4 THIS IS MY FAMILY

TALKING ABOUT FAMILY (USING *HAVE*)

I **have** two sisters. / I **don't have** any sisters.		
She **has** a brother. / She **doesn't have** any brothers.		don't = do not
They **have** a brother. / They **don't have** any brothers.		doesn't = does not
Do you **have** any brothers or sisters?	Yes, I **do**. / No, I **don't**.	
Does she **have** any brothers?	Yes, she **does**. / No, she **doesn't**.	
Do they **have** any cousins?	Yes, they **do**. / No, they **don't**.	

UNIT 5 I LIKE FRUIT!

TALKING ABOUT LIKES AND DISLIKES (USING *LIKE*)

I **like** fruit. I **don't like** vegetables.			
He **likes** popcorn. She **doesn't like** milk.		**Countable**	**Uncountable**
They **like** rice, but they **don't like** sandwiches.		sandwich(**es**)	milk
Do you **like** juice?	Yes, I **do**.	dessert(**s**)	water
	No, I **don't**.	vegetable(**s**)	bread
Does he **like** oranges?	Yes, he **does**.		
	No, he **doesn't**.		

UNIT 6 WHAT TIME DOES CLASS START?

TALKING ABOUT ROUTINES (USING ADVERBS OF FREQUENCY)

What time do you **get up**?	I **always get up** at 7 o'clock.	100%	always
When do you **have breakfast**?	I **usually have breakfast** at 7:30.		usually
	I **often have breakfast** at 6:45.		often
When does he **do his homework**?	**Sometimes** he **does his homework** in the afternoon, and **sometimes** he **does** it at night. He **never does** it in the morning.		sometimes
What time does school **start**?	It **starts** at 8 o'clock.		
When do they **go** to school?	They **go** to school at 7 o'clock.	0%	never

UNIT 7 CAN ELEPHANTS SWIM?

TALKING ABOUT ABILITIES (USING *CAN*)		
I **can** speak two languages. She **can** play the piano.		can't = cannot
Can you swim?	Yes, I **can**. / No, I **can't**.	
What **can** monkeys do?	They **can** climb trees, but they **can't** fly.	
Can he play baseball?	No, he **can't**, but he **can** play tennis.	

UNIT 8 HOW MUCH IS THAT T-SHIRT?

TALKING ABOUT PRICES		
How much is this T-shirt? **How much are** those sneakers?	It's cheap. It's only $20. They're $50.	
I'd like that wallet, please.	Here you are. / Here you go.	I'd = I would
Would you like this hat?	Yes, please. No, thanks. **I'd like** that one.	
Would you like to see these backpacks?	No, thanks. **I'd like to see** those ones, please.	

UNIT 9 WHAT ARE YOU DOING?

TALKING ABOUT WHAT SOMEONE IS DOING (USING PRESENT PROGRESSIVE)	
What **are** you **doing**? What**'s** he **doing**?	I**'m texting**. He**'s checking** his email.
Is she **listening** to music?	**Yes**, she **is**. / **No**, she **isn't**.
Are they **using** the computer?	**Yes**, they **are**. / No, they **aren't**.
Who **are** you **chatting** with?	I**'m chatting** with a friend.

UNIT 10 WHAT'S THE WEATHER LIKE?

TALKING ABOUT WEATHER	
What's the weather **like** today?	**It's** cold.
What's the weather **like** in the summer?	**It's** always hot and dry.
What's the weather **like** in April?	**It's** usually warm, but sometimes it's rainy.
Is it usually cold in the winter?	Yes, **it is.** / No, **it isn't.**
How hot **is** it?	**It's** (about) 30 degrees.
How cold **is** it?	**It's** (about) minus 12 degrees.

UNIT 11 I WENT TO AUSTRALIA!

TALKING ABOUT PAST EVENTS (USING SIMPLE PAST)	
How **was** your vacation?	It **was** amazing!
How **were** the beaches?	They **were** beautiful!
What **did** you **do**?	I **stayed** at home.
	I **swam** in a river.
	I **ate** a lot of good food.
Did you **go** camping?	Yes, I **did.** / No, I **didn't.**
When **did** you **go**?	I went **last summer** / **last week** / **last year**.

UNIT 12 WHAT DID YOU DO FOR NEW YEAR'S?

TALKING ABOUT SPECIAL OCCASIONS (USING PREPOSITIONS OF TIME)	
There was a big festival **during** the winter / the holidays.	
What did you do **on** Friday / July 1st?	We went to a party.
Where did you go **in** August / 2019 / the summer?	I traveled to the Philippines.
Did you go on vacation **for** two weeks / the New Year?	Yes, I did.
	No, I didn't. I stayed at home.

CREDITS

Photo Credits

Art Credits

Text Credits